WHAT
WOULD
Jesus Say?
Biblical Confessions for Teens

Suzette T. Caldwell

ISBN – 978-0-9828041-3-1
Printed in the United States of America
2014 – First Edition

Book design and layout: Jerome Duran – i-dezine-it.com

Scripture references were taken from the New Living Translation version of the Bible unless otherwise indicated.

CMI Publications
6011 West Orem Drive
Houston, TX 77085
(713) 726-2523

Love,

Hebrews 13:20-21

The Lord gave the Word;
great was the company of
those who proclaimed it.

Psalm 68:11

Table Of Contents

Table Of Contents

WHAT WOULD JESUS SAY? BIBLICAL CONFESSIONS FOR TEENS

Dear Teen,

I have prepared this book with you exclusively in mind. This time in your life will be exciting, challenging, fun and sometimes frustrating. Let these Kingdom words, God's recipe for life, help you to excel, achieve, abstain and celebrate in all that you do. Use these Scriptures to encourage and strengthen you. The key to Scripture working for you is in speaking them out loud. When you do, God infuses them with power to work on your behalf and produce His will for your life.

Contrary to what you may think or feel, God loves and empowers teenagers to do mighty things for Him. King David, Esther, Daniel, and Mary, the mother of Jesus, were just a few of the teenagers that God trusted and worked with to do mighty things for Him. Trust God to help and work with you. Jesus Christ loves you and He wants you to "rock" in your life!

God bless you!
Pastor Suzette T. Caldwell

LETTER TO PARENT OR GUARDIAN

What Would Jesus Say will be a blessing to your child(ren). Encourage them to speak aloud the Scriptures I have provided for key areas of their lives. When Scripture is spoken out loud, it is infused with God's power to produce His will for the life of the person who is speaking it. God's Word can be spoken at any time of the day. In our home, Kirbyjon and I confess Scripture over the children before they leave for school in the morning or at bedtime. The Scriptures can also be used to start up family discussions about contemporary issues that young people face daily. When you verbally release the Word for the day expect it to do its job. Psalm 107:20 states the God sent His Word to "...heal us and deliver us from destruction." Say God's Word and watch it change your teen's life.

God bless you!
Pastor Suzette T. Caldwell

INTRODUCTION

Words are very powerful. When spoken, they carry life or death; good news or bad news; fear or faith. They can release a future with hope or a future full of destruction. In Proverbs 18:21, the Bible states that the power of life and death is in our tongue. When we speak words of defeat and doubt, we are literally killing our God-given successful futures. Everything we need for success in life is in God's Word. It is God's will for our lives. We experience God's blessings for our lives through speaking and acting upon His commands. When we are going through life's challenges, the Word of God provides the power, strength, and wisdom to endure and overcome.

In 2004, I declared the Word of God every day when I was diagnosed with breast cancer. Of course, the news was devastating and, like any human person, I cried from the emotional overload and thoughts of the news. I clearly remember the moment that I pulled myself together and decided that I was going to hear what God had to say about the situation. The doctor had given me the facts and I needed to know what the truth said about the facts. I gathered Scriptures on healing and on what God will do when His people are in a crisis.

As I collected these Scriptures, the Holy Spirit instructed me to speak His Word three times a day as if I were taking medicine. God's Word would be the scriptural medicine while taking the natural medicine prescribed by the doctors. You can read more about my testimony in my book, *"Praying to Change Your Life."* The Word of God is medicine that will heal us. As I obeyed His instructions and followed His plan, I am blessed today to say that I am totally cancer-free! Praise God! The same God that healed me can bring life to your situation. Your challenge does not have to be physical; it can be emotional, financial, mental, or spiritual. Whatever the case, the Word of God can change your life.

This book has been written to help you speak life-filled words that will change your life. I want to encourage you to speak these words every day for whatever your situation requires. The more you practice this discipline, the more you will experience God's abundance, joy, peace, and contentment. Speaking and declaring God's Word is simple. You can do this!

I have written God's Word into biblical confessions that are going to spring to life within you. These Kingdom Words will bring change, so speak life and enjoy what God intended for you and your family.

PRAISE GOD!

Psalm 150:6 says that every living creature is to praise God; that includes you! Before you listen to your favorite "jams," start your day blessing God your Father, Jesus your Savior, and the Holy Spirit, your Eternal Friend. By the way, if your favorite "jam" conflicts with God's Word, you "jam" up the Word in your world.

David said in Psalm 34:1, "I will bless the Lord at all times, His praise will always be in my mouth." Our triune God loves to be appreciated and adored. Tell Him how much you love Him and don't forget to say "thank you" for all He does in your life. Now, rap, sing, or speak the following Scriptures and look forward to having a great day. The Lord deserves your praise!

SCRIPTURES TO SAY!

I will praise the Lord (God the Father, Jesus Christ, and the Holy Spirit) at all times. I will constantly speak His praises.

Psalm 34:1

Lord, everything comes from You; everything happens through You; everything ends up in You. All glory and praise belong to You forever! Amen.

Romans 11:36 (The Message and NKJV)

Lord of Heaven's Armies, You are holy, holy, holy. The whole earth is filled with Your glory!

Isaiah 6:3

Your throne, O God, endures forever and ever. Your royal power is expressed in righteousness. You love what is right and hate what is wrong. Therefore, God, Your God, has anointed You (Jesus), pouring out the oil of joy on You (Jesus) more than anyone else.

Hebrews 1:8-9

God! Let the cosmos praise your wonderful ways. Let the choir of holy angels sing anthems to your faithful ways! If I were to search high and low or scan skies and land, I would find nothing and no one quite like You. The holy angels are in awe of You. You loom immense and august over everyone around You. God of the Angel Armies, who is like You? You are powerful and faithful from every angle.

Psalm 89:5-8 (The Message)

We praise You, Lord! Let everyone on earth bless Your holy Name forever and ever!

Psalm 145:21

O Lord, Your name endures forever. Lord, Your fame is known to every generation. For You give justice to Your people and have compassion on Your servants. The idols of the nations are merely things of silver and gold, shaped by human hands.

Psalm 135:13-15

Blessed be the Name of the Lord now and forever. Everywhere – from east to west – praise the Name of the Lord. Lord, You are high above the nations; Your glory is higher than the heavens.

Psalm 113:2-4

Sovereign Lord, You have made the heavens and earth by Your strong hand and powerful arm. Nothing is too hard for You! You performed miraculous signs and wonders in the land of Egypt–things still remembered this day. And You have continued to do great miracles in Israel and all around the world. You have made Your Name famous to this day.

Jeremiah 32:17, 20

Lord, You are the Rock; Your deeds are perfect. Everything You do is just and fair. You are a faithful God who does no wrong. You are just and upright!

Deuteronomy 32:2-4

ASKING THE LORD FOR FORGIVENESS

As you grow into adulthood, you are going to make mistakes. There are some mistakes that are considered sins against God. Sin is a deliberate act of defiance. When a person sins, they are acting against what God has said is right and true. Examples of sin include lying, disobedience to parents and persons of authority, gossiping, selfishness, jealousy, premarital sex and drunkenness. God wants the best for your life. Jesus died on the cross to free you from the bondage of sin. When you sin (all of us sin at times), be quick to ask for forgiveness. Be serious about your request and Jesus will forgive you and hit the reset button in your life. You will be released from the crippling, destructive power of sin. Be free! Live free! Stay free!

SCRIPTURES TO SAY!

I confess my sins to You, Lord (**say the specific sin(s) aloud**). I will stop trying to hide my guilt. Lord, I confess my rebellion to You (**confess how you have rebelled against God**). Merciful Father, I believe You have forgiven me. All my guilt is gone. Praise the Lord!

Psalm 32:5

Loving Father, have mercy on me because of your unfailing love. Because of your great compassion, blot out the stain of my sins.

Psalm 51:1

Wash me clean from my guilt. Purify me from my sin. I recognize that I have rebelled against You. This stays on my mind night and day. Lord, forgive me.

Psalm 51:2-3

Gracious Father, if you purify me from my sins, I will be clean. Wash me and I will be whiter than snow.

Psalm 51:8-9

I will put away wicked ways and banish the thoughts of doing wrong. Father, I am turning toward You to receive Your mercy and forgiveness generously.

Isaiah 55:7

Almighty God, create in me a clean heart and renew a loyal spirit within me. Do not banish me from your presence and please don't take your Holy Spirit from me.

Psalm 51:10-11

My tongue will not devise destruction, nor, like a sharp razor, work deceitfully. I will love good more than evil and speak righteousness more than lies.

Psalm 52:2-3

Today, I confess my sins knowing that God is faithful and just to forgive me of my sins and cleanse me of unrighteousness.

I John 1:9

What a joy it is to know that my disobedience is forgiven and my sin is put out of sight. My record of sin has been cleared of guilt and I can live my life in complete honesty!

Psalm 32:1-2

BUILDING YOUR FAITH

Hebrews 11:6 says that it is impossible to please God without faith. It is essential for living in God's Kingdom. Once you accept Jesus Christ as your Lord and Savior, you receive a measure of faith that will grow as you learn how to follow Christ. Speak the following Scriptures over yourself and expect it to help your life. By faith, you will do all things through Christ!

SCRIPTURES TO SAY!

Faith is the confidence that what I hope for will actually happen. It gives me assurance about things I cannot see.

Hebrews 11:1

It is impossible to please God without faith. I believe that God exists and that He rewards those who sincerely seek Him.

Hebrews 11:6

I believe that Jesus is the Christ and I am a child of God. I love the Father and I love His children, too because I love and obey His commandments.

I John 5:1-2

Jesus is Lord! I believe in my heart that God has raised Him from the dead. I know that I am saved.

Romans 10:9

I believe that with God, nothing is impossible!
Luke 1:37

I believe that there is nothing too hard for God!
Jeremiah 32:27

I will demonstrate my faith by doing good deeds.
James 2:18

I am more than a conqueror through Him who loved me.
Romans 8:37

I rely only on the power of the Holy Spirit. I will not trust in human wisdom, but only in the power of God.
I Corinthians 2:4-5

I am not ashamed of the Gospel of Christ, for it is the power of God for the salvation of everyone who believes.
Romans 1:16

I have been made right with God by my faith in

Jesus Christ, not in obeying the law.

Galatians 2:16

Because of my faith, Christ has brought me into a place of undeserved privilege where I now stand, and I confidently and joyfully look forward to sharing God's glory.

Romans 5:2

I will keep my conscience clear by clinging to my faith in Christ.

I Timothy 1:19

I confess that I am defeating this evil world through my faith.

I John 5:4

I commit to building my faith daily by positioning myself to hear the Word of God.

Romans 10:17

FORGIVING FAMILY, FRIENDS AND ENEMIES

When your feelings are hurt by people, it is important to forgive them quickly. When you don't forgive, it is like drinking poison and expecting someone else to die. You will always be the person who is most affected by unforgiveness. Matthew 6:14 commands us to forgive others if we want to be forgiven by the Lord. Don't hold grudges. Let it go and let the Lord fight your battles. In the meantime, keep your head up, throw back your shoulders, and put a smile on your face. You're too blessed to be stressed.

SCRIPTURES TO SAY!

Jesus says I must forgive. So, I will forgive *(names)*, even if they wrong me seven times a day and each time returns again asking for forgiveness.

Luke 17:4

I will love my enemies and pray for those who persecute me. I will let the Lord fight my battles.

Matthew 5:44
Psalm 3:7

I will forgive *(name)* who have sinned against me and my Heavenly Father will forgive me.

Matthew 6:14

I will let not evil (unforgiveness) conquer me, but I will conquer evil (unforgiveness) by doing good.

Romans 12:21

I will put away all bitterness, rage, anger, quarreling, and slander, as well as all types of evil behavior. Instead, I will be kind, tenderhearted and forgiving to others *(name)*, just as God through Christ has forgiven me.

Ephesians 4:31,32

I can do all things, including forgiving the person(s) who hurt me, through Christ who gives me the strength.

Philippians 4:13

I will not think about the negative, but I will fix my thoughts on what is true, and honorable, and right, and pure, and lovely, and admirable, and excellent, and worth of praise.

Philippians 4:8

Lord, help me to forgive. (Take a moment and ask the Holy Spirit to show you names or faces of people you need to forgive. As He shows you, say aloud, "I forgive <u>name of person(s)</u>." Now trust the Lord the heal any wounds in your soul caused by unforgiveness.)

Matthew 11:28

HONORING AND RESPECTING PARENTS

Your parents are a gift from God. They will love you unconditionally. Always honor your parents, especially in the presence of your friends. You might become impatient with them sometimes, but you must respect them. When you don't agree with them, pray and ask the Holy Spirt to help you to understand their viewpoint. Don't forget to ask God to bless your parents. If you respect and honor your parents you can count on living a long life.

SCRIPTURES TO SAY!

I will honor my father and mother, so that I will live a long, full life in the land of the Lord, my God is giving me.

Exodus 20:12

I will honor (respect, love and obey) my mother and father, for this is God's first commandment with a promise.

Ephesians 6:2

As I honor my mother and father, all things will go well for me and I will have a long life on the earth.

Ephesians 6:3

I will never pay back evil with more evil. I will do things in such a way that my parents can see that I am honorable. I will do all that I can to live in peace with my parents.

Romans 12:17-18

I choose to obey my parents because I belong to

the Lord, and this is the right thing to do.

Ephesians 6:1

I will forgive my parents because Jesus Christ has forgiven me.

Matthew 6:14

I will listen to my father, who gave me life, and I won't despise my mother when she is old.

Proverbs 23:22

I will listen when my father corrects me and I will not neglect (ignore) my mother's instructions.

Proverbs 1:8

OVERCOMING FEAR

So many people miss out on an exciting, full and satisfying life because of fear. It is a part of living, but it must not be allowed to be in control of your life. When you are afraid, whether it be fear of the dark; fear of taking a test; or fear of being successful, tell Jesus and He will replace your fear with His confidence, strength and courage. In Jesus Christ, you are safe and sound. Relax!!! God has got your back.

SCRIPTURES TO SAY!

God has not given me a spirit of fear, but of power and of love and of a sound mind.

II Timothy 1:7 NKJV

Because I trust the Lord I am safe and secure. He is a refuge for all of His children.

Proverbs 14:26

I will not be afraid, for God is with me. I will not be discouraged, for the Lord is my God. He will strengthen me and help me. He will hold me up with His victorious right hand.

Isaiah 41:10

I will wait patiently for the Lord. I will be brave and courageous. Yes! I will wait patiently for the Lord.

Psalm 27:14

I confidently confess that the Lord is my helper. I will have no fear.

Hebrews 13:6

When I walk through the darkest valley, I will not be afraid, for the Lord is close beside me. His rod and staff will comfort and protect me.

Psalm 23:4

Lord, You are my rock, my fortress, and my Savior. You are my rock, in whom I find protection.

II Samuel 22:2

Lord, You are my shield, the power that saves me, and my place of safety. You are my refuge, my Savior, the One who saves me from violence. Father, I need your help!

II Samuel 22:3

Whoever fights me will fail. For the Lord is with me and He will take care of me.

Jeremiah 1:19

OVERCOMING HURT AND DISAPPOINTMENT

Sometimes life just hurts and can be plain disappointing. But, that is no reason to give up. When you have been hurt or disappointed, step back, take a breath and calm yourself. Don't be quick to retaliate and hurt someone else. Talk to your parents, your youth pastor or even a teacher that you trust about how you are feeling. Don't be afraid to cry. The Lord will catch your tears. While the pain may seem like it will never go away, be assured that the Lord will take away any embarrassment, humiliation or shame.

SCRIPTURES TO SAY!

Father, God, You are my shepherd who feeds, guides and shields me. In You, I have everything I need. Help me to lie down in fresh tender green pastures. Lead me beside still and restful waters. Refresh and restore my life and lead me in the path of righteousness for Your name's sake.

Psalm 23:1-3

Lord, I will lean on, trust in and be confident in You with all of my heart and mind. I will not rely on my own insight, understanding [or feelings]. In all of my ways [and everything I do], I will recognize and acknowledge You and I will trust You to direct and make my path straight and plain.

Proverbs 3:4-6 AMP

Jesus, although my life appears to be going through Death Valley, I will not be afraid because I know You are walking beside me. Your trusty shepherd's crook makes me feel secure.

Psalm 23:4 The Message

I will wait on the Lord to help me. I will be brave and of good courage and He will strengthen my heart.

Psalm 27:14

I will not get tired of doing what is good because I know that at the right time I will reap a harvest of blessing if I don't give up.

Galatians 6:9

I will not worry about anything; instead, pray about everything. I will tell God what I need and thank Him for all He has done. *(Now, talk to God about what you need and thank Him for what He has done in your life.)*

Philippians 4:6

I will forgive those who have hurt me so that I can be forgiven.

Matthew 6:14

Lord, look at me and help me! I am all alone

and in big trouble. Keep watch over me and keep me out of trouble; don't let me down when I run to you.

Psalm 25:16,20 The Message

If God is for me, who can be against me!

Romans 8:31

OVERCOMING THE NEED TO BE VALIDATED BY PEOPLE

Every normal person wants to be validated or affirmed as a member of a family or community. You, as a teenager, are not an exception. The good news is when you are a believer, you are validated and affirmed by Jesus Christ! Nothing or nobody can deny you of that validation and affirmation - unless you give them your permission.

The challenge is both the enemy and your 'haters' will attempt to tempt you to seek validation from persons and things that are actually designed to diminish and destroy you. It is the enemy's job to tempt you. It is your job to resist the temptation. You can do all things through Christ! You are affirmed and validated by God through Jesus Christ.

SCRIPTURES TO SAY!

I, *(plug in your name),* am fearfully and wonderfully made by the Lord God Almighty Himself!

Psalm 139:14

I, *(name)*, am made in God's image, according to His likeness. I have dominion over EVERYTHING God has made.

Genesis 1:26

I, *(name)*, am created in God's image as a (male/female) to give God glory and honor.

Genesis 1:27

God loves me, *(name)*, so much that He sacrificed His only Son so I can live both abundantly, right now, and everlastingly with Him forever when I choose to believe in Jesus.

John 3:16, John 10:10

Jesus Christ's love for me is so great that He

willingly gave His life for me. Jesus is my friend!

John 10:10-11, James 2:23

I, *(name)*, am loved by God so much and I am so special in His sight that there is nothing ever created that can separate me from the love of God which is in Jesus Christ.

Romans 8:38-39

As an adopted son/daughter of God through Jesus Christ, His grace insists that I am accepted in the eyes of God!

Ephesians 1:5-6

I was made a little lower than God Himself and He has crowned me with glory and honor.

Psalm 8:6

PEER PRESSURE: FEELING CONFIDENT ABOUT BEING "YOU"

At this point in your life, the opinions, values, and beliefs of your friends seem to be very important. You must remember that God created you and you are uniquely special. Don't be pressured by what other people think or say about you. Let your gifts, talents, and personality reflect the love of Christ. Just be you because everyone else is already taken.

SCRIPTURES TO SAY!

I am God's masterpiece. He has created me brand new in Christ Jesus, so that I can do the good things He planned for me long ago.

Ephesians 2:10

O God, how precious are Your thoughts about me. They cannot be numbered!

Psalm 139:17

Lord, You made all the delicate, inner parts of my body and knit me together in my mother's womb. Thank You for making me so wonderfully complex! Your workmanship is marvelous. I choose to believe this about myself.

Psalm 139:13-14

Lord, I confess that You are my Father. I am the clay, and You are the potter. I am formed by Your hand. You made me; You created me. I am special!

Isaiah 64:8

Lord, You do not see things the way people see them. People judge by outward appearances, but You look at my heart. I will trust You with all my heart. I will not lean to my own understanding. I will believe in myself.

I Samuel 16:17, Proverbs 3:5

As a young woman, I will not be concerned (focused) about the outward beauty of fancy hairstyles, expensive jewelry, or beautiful clothes. Instead, I will clothe myself with the beauty that comes from within, the unfading beauty of a gentle and quiet spirit, which is so precious to God.

I Peter 3:4

As a young man, I will guard clear thinking and common sense with my life. Not for one minute will I lose sight of them. Clear thinking and common sense will keep my soul alive and well; and I will be fit and attractive to people around me.

Proverbs 3:21-23

I will love the Lord, my God, with all my

heart, soul, mind, and all my strength. Equally important, I will love my neighbor as I love myself. No other commandment is greater than these.

Mark 12:30

God has reconciled me to Himself through the death of Christ in His physical body. As a result, He has brought me into His own presence, and I am holy and blameless as I stand before Him without a single fault. When I make a mistake or commit a sin I will ask God to forgive me and I believe that He will forgive me and cleanse me of all unrighteousness.

Colossians 1:22
I John 1:9

I will be kind to others, tenderhearted, and forgive others, just as God in Christ has forgiven me.

Ephesians 4:32

I will listen to the commands of the Lord, my God, which He has given me (through Scripture) and I will carefully obey them. As a result, the Lord will make me the head and not the tail, and I will always be on top and never on the bottom.

Deuteronomy 28:13

I can do everything through Christ; who gives me strength. That means I can do well in my academics, athletics, and the arts. I can be a responsible son, daughter, student, friend, employee, leader, and citizen in my community.

Philippians 4:13

POWER WORDS TO BLESS A TEEN'S ACTIVITIES (INCLUDING ACADEMICS, ATHLETICS AND THE ARTS)

Your life is extremely busy. You are expected to excel in academics, athletics, the arts, and community service. Additionally, you are expected to do chores and, sometimes, work to help out at home. All of these expectations can be overwhelming. Gone are the days when teens could come home from school, eat a snack, finish homework and hang out with friends in the neighborhood. Pray the following Scriptures to encourage and empower yourself to accomplish your responsibilities.

SCRIPTURES TO SAY!

I can do everything through Christ who gives me strength.

Philippians 4:13

As a believer, I have the mind of Christ, therefore, I can think, learn, and focus like Him.

I Corinthians 2:16

God shows no partiality; just like He blessed Samson with great strength, I believe He will bless me.

Ephesians 6:9, Judges 13-16)

God has not given me a spirit of fear, but power, love and sound mind. I can do this!

I Timothy 1:7

I am more than a conqueror through Jesus Christ who loved me.

Romans 8:37

I rely on the power of the Holy Spirit. I will not trust in human wisdom, but in the power of God!

1 Corinthians 2:4-5

I will trust in the Lord with all of my heart. I will not depend on my own understanding, but I will seek God's will in all I do and depend on Him to show me which path to take.

Proverbs 3:5-6

As a child of God, I will obey my parents because it is the right thing to do. I will honor my mother and father and show them respect. As a result, my life will be successful and I will live a long time.

Ephesians 6:1-3

I am a gift from the Lord. I am like arrows in the hand of a warrior.

Psalm 127:3-4

PROTECTION

In Christ, you are always protected. Don't worry about your life. God will watch over you and keep you from hurt, harm and danger.

SCRIPTURES TO SAY!

Because I live in the shelter of the Most High, I will find rest in the shadow of the Almighty. This I declare about the Lord: He alone is my refuge and my place of safety. He is my God and I trust Him.

Psalm 91:1-2

I will rejoice as I take refuge in God. I will sing His praises forever. I will trust the Lord to spread His protection over me. I will love the Lord and be filled with His joy.

Psalm 5:11

The Lord is my hiding place. He protects me from trouble and surrounds me with songs of victory.

Psalm 32:7

May the Lord answer my cry in times of trouble. May the name of the God of Jacob keep me safe from all harm. May He send me help from His

sanctuary and strengthen me from Jerusalem.
Psalm 20:1-2

The Lord is faithful; He will strengthen me and
guard me from the evil one!
II Thessalonians 3:3

Jesus has given me eternal life, and I will never
perish. No one can snatch me from Jesus.
John 10:28

The temptations in my life are no different
from what others experience. God is faithful!
He will not allow the temptation to be more
than I can stand. When I am tempted, He will
show me a way out, so that I can endure.
I Corinthians 10:13

The Lord is my light and salvation, so why
should I be afraid? The Lord is my fortress,
protecting me from danger, so why should
I tremble? When evil people come to devour
me, when my enemies and foes attack me, they
will stumble and fall. Though a mighty army
surrounds me, my heart will not be afraid. Even

if I am attacked, I will remain confident.

Psalm 27:1-3

The Name of the Lord is a strong tower. I (the righteous) will run to it and find safety!

Proverbs 18:10

Arise, O Lord! Rescue me, my God! Slap all my enemies in the face! Shatter the teeth of the wicked! Victory comes from You, O Lord. May You bless Your people.

Psalm 3:7-8

The Lord is my strength and my shield. I will trust Him with all of my heart. He helps me, and my heart is filled with joy. I will burst out in songs of thanksgiving.

Psalm 28:7

Even if my father and mother abandon me, the Lord will hold me close.

Psalm 28:10

SALVATION

Jesus wants you to know Him as Lord and Savior. He came to earth so that you may have an abundant life in Him. There are so many distractions in the world that are trying to draw you away from God's love. As you speak these Scriptures, expect the power of God to bring you closer to Christ. Jesus understands you because he was once a teenager. Let Him become your best friend. He will always be with you.

SCRIPTURES TO SAY!

I confess with my mouth that Jesus is Lord and I believe in my heart that God raised Him from the dead. Therefore, I am saved! HalleluYAH! (Praise God)

Romans 10:9

I have been united with Christ Jesus. I was once far away from God, but now I have been brought near to God through the blood of Christ.

Ephesians 2:13

As I come close to God, He comes close to me. My sins are then washed away and my heart is purified! My loyalty is not divided between God and the world.

James 4:8

I believe that even before God made the world, He loved me and chose me to be holy and without fault in His eyes. He decided in advance to adopt me into His own family through Jesus Christ because it gave Him great pleasure. Hallel YAH! (Praise God)

Ephesians 1:4-5

I believe that God has come to save me. I will trust in Him and not be afraid. He is my strength and song.

Isaiah 12:2

Because I have believed and accepted Jesus as my Lord and Savior, I have the right to be called a child of God.

John 1:12

I belong to Christ, so I have become a new person. My old life is gone; my new life has begun!

II Corinthians 5:17

I believe that God loved the world so much that He gave His one and only Son, so that everyone who believes in Him will not perish, but have eternal life.   God sent His Son into the world, not to judge the world, but to save the world through Him.

John 3:16-17

My salvation is in no one else but Jesus Christ! God has given no other name under heaven by which we must be saved.

Acts 4:12

All praise to God, the Father of our Lord Jesus Christ, who has blessed me with every spiritual blessing in the heavenly realms because I am united with Christ.

Ephesians 1:3

I believe in the Lord Jesus; therefore, I know I am saved! I confess that everyone in my household will be saved.

Acts 16:31

The wages of sin is death, but the free gift of God is eternal life through Christ Jesus our Lord.

Romans 6:23

God saved me by His grace when I believed. I can't take credit for this; it is a gift from God!

Ephesians 2:8

Salvation is not a reward for the good things we have done, so none of us can boast about it. I am God's masterpiece. He has created me anew in Christ Jesus so I can do the good things He planned for me long ago.

Ephesians 2:9

Jesus Christ is the Way, the Truth and the Life. No one can come to the Father except through Him.

John 14:6

God, our Savior, revealed His kindness and love when He saved us, not because of the righteous things we've done, but because of His mercy. He has washed away our sins, and given us a new birth and new life through the Holy Spirit.

Titus 3:4-5

SEX AND TEMPTATION

As a Christian, how do you handle sex? Sex was created by God and placed within marriage. It is a blessing that He has given as a gift to humanity for the purpose of developing love between a husband and a wife and to produce children who will grow to be productive citizens in our world.

The world is trying to convince you that sex is OK before marriage. In the Bible, Scripture instructs single people not to have sex before marriage. When you have sex outside of marriage you create a soul tie that will produce confusion, disappointment and heartache. Do the right thing and follow God's plan. Sex may be hard to resist, in spite of what you see and hear in the media, but the Holy Spirit will help you. If you find yourself being tempted, ask the Holy Spirit to give you the strength to walk away and wait until you marry. You can do this!

SCRIPTURES TO PRAY

My body is the temple (house) of the Holy Spirit, who lives in me and was given to me by God. I do not belong to myself. I belong to God. Jesus Christ bought me with a high price. So, I must honor God with my body.

I Corinthians 6:19-20

I will not sin against my own body. I will **RUN** from sexual sin, (premarital sex, adultery, homosexuality, bisexuality, transsexuality and bestiality).

I Corinthians 6:18

I am fearfully and wonderfully made by God, therefore, I will respect Him by respecting myself.

Psalm 139:14

I will not indulge in sexual sins, such as idolatry, adultery, prostitution, homosexuality, stealing, greed, drunkenness, abuse or cheating people. I am only fooling myself if I think I will inherit the Kingdom of God while doing these things. As a follower of Christ I have been cleansed of these sins; I have been made holy; and I am in right standing with God through the Holy Spirit.

I Corinthians 6:9-11

Praise the Lord! I can never escape from the Holy Spirit. I will never get away from His presence. Therefore, if I choose to participate in premarital sex, Jesus will see me. I will not embarrass Him or myself.

Psalm 139:7

God is my refuge and my strength and He is ready to help in times of trouble (including when I am tempted to have sex).

Psalm 46:1

I will not let sin control the way I live and I will not give into sinful desires.

Romans 6:12

I will not let any part of my body become an instrument of evil to serve sin. Instead, I will give myself completely to God.

Romans 6:13a

I am no longer considered (spiritually) dead, but I am alive in Jesus Christ and I will use my whole body as a vessel of honor to do what is right for the glory of God.

Ephesians 2:1, 2 Timothy 2:21

Since Jesus Christ overcame suffering and testing (temptation), I believe that He is able to help me when I am tempted.

Hebrews 2:18

TAKING ACADEMIC TESTS AND EXAMS

God wants you to do well in school. He blessed Daniel, Meshach, Shadrach and Abednego (Daniel 1) to be excellent students. Study hard, take good notes, ask questions, keep up with your homework and visit your teachers regularly. Always do your best. You may not always make an "A," but you can always do your best. You are smart, gifted, and God's best. Go for it!

SCRIPTURES TO SAY!

As I study for my final exams, I will confess God's word over my life and meditate on it day and night, so that I will be careful to do everything that is written in it. Then, I will be prosperous and have good success on my exams.

Joshua 1:8

I will not be anxious and worry about my exams; instead, I will pray about them. I will tell God what I need *(take a moment to tell God what you need help with as you study for your exams);* and thank Him for all He has done *(tell God "thank you" for three things He helped you with while in school this year).* Then I will experience God's peace, which exceeds anything I can understand. His peace will guard my heart and mind because I live in Christ Jesus.

Philippians 4:6-7

God has not given me a spirit of fear, so I will not be afraid of my exams. I have the power to complete my exams; I have the capacity to love my teachers and fellow students; and my mind is sound enough to think, understand and reproduce what I have learned during the school year.

II Timothy 1:7

I will be strong and of good courage concerning my final exams. I will not be fearful because the Lord, my God, will go with me. He will never leave me nor forsake me.

Deuteronomy 31:6

I was created in the image of God and I have the mind of Christ. Therefore, I can learn, comprehend, think and recall the subjects I have learned this school year.

Genesis 1:26, I Corinthians 2:16

Just like Daniel, Shadrach, Meshach and Abednego, I confess that God is giving me an unusual aptitude for understanding all of my class studies. Therefore, I will excel on all of my exams because I can do all things through Jesus

Christ who strengthens me. Peace, be still in my mind, body and soul!

Daniel 1:17, Philippians 4:13, Mark 4:39

As I prepare for my final exams, I am confident that God has gifted me in all wisdom and knowledge and I am quick to understand.

Daniel 1:4

I declare that God's wisdom reigns in my heart and knowledge fills me with joy.

Proverbs 2:10

I am blessed because I believe in Jesus Christ. As a result, the favor of God surrounds me and protects my life.

Psalm 5:12

I will commit my exams to the Lord, therefore I will be successful!

Proverbs 16:3

WORDS TO RELEASE STRESS AND BRING PEACE

Life can really stress you out. I have great news for you! Jesus will release the stress. As you say the following Scriptures, relax, take a deep breath, and allow God's word to bring peace.

SCRIPTURES TO SAY!

The Lord keeps me in perfect peace because I trust Him and my thoughts are fixed on Him.

Isaiah 26:3

I will trust in the Lord always, for the Lord God is my eternal Rock.

Isaiah 26:4

Jesus has given me the gift of peace of mind and heart; it's a gift the world cannot give. Therefore, I will not be troubled or afraid.

John 14:27

The Lord is my shepherd. He provides all that I need.

Psalm 23:1

May God give me more and more mercy, peace, and love.

Jude 2

I will not let my heart be troubled. I will trust

in God and Jesus Christ.

John 14:1

May the Lord bless and protect me. May the Lord smile on me and be gracious to me. May the Lord show His favor and give me peace.

Numbers 6:25-26

The peace of God guards my heart and mind as I live in Christ Jesus; therefore, I will not worry about anything. Instead, I will pray about everything.

Philippians 4:6-7

In peace I will lie down and sleep, for you alone, O Lord, will keep me safe.

Psalm 4:8

I can do all things through Christ who gives me strength.

Philippians 4:13

I am like a tree planted by the rivers of water bearing fruit (being productive) each season and whose leaves never wither. I will prosper in all that I do.

Psalm 1:3

I will submit my life to God and expect peace; then, things will go well with me.

Job 22:21